Other books by Tracey Turner

The Disgusting Dictionary
The Who's Who of Horrors
The Yuk Factor

THE BOOK OF BIG EXCUSES

THE BOOK OF **BIG** EXCUSES

Tracey Turner

Illustrated by Sally Kindberg

A division of Hachette Children's Books

'A bad excuse is better than none.'
Proverb

On the other hand …

'Bad excuses are worse than none.'
Thomas Fuller

Contents

IT WASN'T MY FAULT...

Chapter 1
Excuses, Excuses …

We all make excuses from time to time. In fact, when you think about it, we couldn't live without them: excuses for keeping someone waiting, missing a deadline, cancelling a date, having an accident, behaving badly or just being a lazy slacker. In this book you'll find hundreds of excuses for lots of different things, from being late for school to flying an unauthorised garden chair over Los Angeles.

Some of these excuses are bizarre but true, some are

obvious attempts to weasel a way out of blame and others are explanations for strange behaviour. They involve all sorts of unlikely events: falling monks, giant clowns on railway lines and mushy peas on motorways. And all sorts of unlikely animals: monkeys, ferrets, ostriches, angry moose, exploding pigeons and mating herons all have an unexpected part to play.

From some of these excuses you might learn valuable lessons. For example …

- ☞ you're unlikely to get away with pretending to be dead

- ☞ it's better to dump someone with no excuse at all than to tell them it's because they only like early Radiohead

- ☞ sometimes, giving a genuine excuse is far more embarrassing than saying nothing

- ☞ pretending to be an answering machine is never going to be convincing

☞ never attempt to eat your underpants under
   any circumstances

More wisdom, and quite a lot
of complete stupidity, awaits
you. Next time you need to
think up an excuse,
contemplate the following
... and maybe think about
keeping your mouth shut.

Quotation
'We have forty million
reasons for failure, but
not a single excuse.'
Rudyard Kipling

Chapter 2
Sorry I'm Late But...

There's an obvious reason for being late: not leaving early enough. That's not much of an excuse though, so people try to find better ones. The most common are sick children, heavy traffic and public transport (which has a whole chapter of its own from page 30). But here are some more imaginative efforts ...

Turning up late

☞ A writer was due to have his first meeting with an editor, so you would have thought he'd try to make a good impression. But the time set for the meeting came and went, and the editor became worried. Two hours later she managed to track him down. He told her that the wind had blown over his alarm clock and he'd overslept. In fact, alarm clocks are often to blame for people being late – they are unpredictable things, often faulty, and at the mercy of passing pets (see the Top Twenty Lateness Excuses on page 19).

☞ An Australian girl turned up late for school wearing a pair of trainers instead of school shoes. She produced a note for her teacher that read, 'Please excuse Sarah for being out of uniform as a dingo ate her school shoes.'

☞ On only her fourth day at a new job, one woman was an hour and a half late because, she claimed, she couldn't find the building.

☞ An office worker explained to his boss that when he woke up a window cleaner was cleaning his bedroom windows. Offering way too much

Quotation
'One year ago today, the time for excuse-making has come to an end.'
George W Bush

information, the man explained that he was late because he was sleeping naked and had to wait to get up until the window cleaner had finished.

☞ Sometimes people claim they are late because they've been involved in an act of heroism. One woman claimed to have helped deliver a baby on her way to work (even though she had no medical training), and another claimed his neighbour's house was on fire and he had helped to put it out.

☞ For three years running, an office worker was an hour late on the Monday morning after the change to summer daylight-saving time.

☞ An art student was half an hour late back to class because, he said, he'd had to queue for a temporary pass into the college building with a friend who'd lost his ID card. The

Quotation

'Pessimism is an excuse for not trying and a guarantee to a personal failure.'
Bill Clinton

teacher, quite reasonably, asked why he couldn't have gone straight to class instead of queueing with his friend. The student replied, 'I did, I just walked very slowly so he could catch up,' and demonstrated shuffling slowly along to clarify his point.

Top Twenty Lateness Excuses

Some are lame, others are strange and some are both ...

1 *'I'm locked in a public toilet and no one is around to let me out.'*

2 *'I was peed on by a dog while waiting at the bus stop and had to go home and change.'*

3 *'My snake escaped.'*

4 *'My cat unplugged my alarm clock.'*

5 *'My dog turned off my alarm clock.'*

6 *'My baby turned off my alarm clock.'*

7 *'There was a bird stuck in the chimney.'*

8 *'I realised my shoes clashed horribly with my*

skirt and had to go home and change.'

9 'I helped an old lady across the road then had to stay and chat.'

10 'There was an angry wasp caught in my hair.'

11 'I couldn't remember where I parked the car.'

12 'I was cornered by an aggressive swan on the canal towpath.'

13 'I had to take my cat to the dentist.'

14 'A van crashed into the front of my house.'

15 'The rearview mirror in my car fell off.'

16 'I was saving abandoned puppies.'

17 'Hair emergency.'

18 'We had to wait for a large herd of cows crossing the road.'

'*I was pursued by a swarm of bees.*'

 '*I was being followed by six ducklings so I had to lead them back home and call the vet.*'

☞ When an employee was an hour late for work his boss phoned his home number and was told by his wife that he'd left for work at the usual time. The man turned up a few minutes later, apologised and explained that he'd overslept. Puzzled, his boss told him what his wife had said. So the man claimed that some time during the night he had fallen out of bed – when his wife answered the phone she looked over at his side of the bed and assumed he must have left for work. The real reason was that he'd been for a job interview at a rival company – and forgotten to warn his wife.

☞ A student was going to be late for college on the morning of an important test because she was stuck behind a slow-moving tractor. She got out, stopped the tractor and asked the driver to write her a note, which she handed to the lecturer when she arrived twenty minutes late.

☞ A teacher was late for work and knew that the head teacher was very strict about time keeping. She also knew that the head was an animal lover and owned a horse. So she phoned the school and explained that there was a horse loose on a busy road, so she was going to try and help catch it and save its life. The head swallowed the story and didn't mark the teacher late that day.

☞ A grey squirrel caused a power cut in Toronto one work day morning when it chewed through a wire, was electrocuted and caused a short in the system. As well as shutting down the electricity supply, causing all sorts of important documents to be 'lost' and giving everyone an excuse for an extra long tea break, traffic lights were affected, which meant major traffic jams. Hundreds of people were instantly provided with a good excuse.

Quotation

'Your letter of excuses has arrived. I receive the letter but do not admit the excuses except in courtesy, as when a man treads on your toes and begs your pardon – the pardon is granted, but the joint aches, especially if there is a corn upon it.'
Lord Byron

☞ A dog was responsible for lots of people being late for school and work in Wales when it took a pee against a pylon. The dog cocked its leg, there was an explosion and power was cut off to 148 houses for five hours. The pylon had been faulty so it wasn't really the poor dog's fault – it had to be treated for burns but made a full recovery.

Missing deadlines

☞ Computer failures seem to happen to students a lot. Strange malfunctions that wipe

entire hard drives are
much more common
than you would have
thought. One university

Quotation
'Don't make excuses
make good.'
Elbert Hubbard

student told his professor that he'd been
emailing him work all term to an address that
he had just found out wasn't correct, but that
hadn't bounced the messages. Of course, his
work hadn't been saved and he needed time
to do it again.

☞ Back in the days before computers were
common, there was far more opportunity for
'lost homework' excuses. Violent gusts of
wind swept neatly written pages off
windowsills, or even out of students' hands.
Homework was dropped into puddles where
it disintegrated in a matter of seconds. Pets
ate it, or even (in one genuine case) had a
terrible case of the runs all over it.

☞ IT departments have been known to make
mistakes. All employees in one company had
to send an email to everyone in their address

books informing them that they'd lost all emails, both sent and received, for a period of just over a week, and that it was impossible to retrieve them. Thanks to the IT department, everyone in the company was instantly handed a cast-iron excuse for all sorts of things they should have done but hadn't.

☞ An Argentinian man took his car to a garage for some minor repairs in 2000. In 2006 he was still waiting for it. The garage owner made a series of excuses, including his aunt's death and a burglary in his shop. The man ended up suing the garage in desperation.

☞ The Victorian writer Samuel Taylor Coleridge was always late with his work. His epic poem *Kubla Khan* was never finished – Coleridge claimed that this was because 'a person from Porlock' interrupted the dream he was having, which was the inspiration for the poem. He was late replying to letters, too. His long list of excuses to one friend read, 'I should have written you long ere this . . . my Health has been very bad, and remains so – a nervous Affection from my right temple to the extremity of my right shoulder almost distracted me, & made the frequent use of Laudanum absolutely necessary. And since I have subdued this, a Rheumatic Complaint in the back of my Head & Shoulders, accompanied with sore throat ...' (continues for some pages).

☞ A man in Zagreb, Croatia, returned a library book 40 years late. During a library fine amnesty, the man handed in the book, which he'd borrowed in 1967, and explained that he'd never got round to reading Rudyard Kipling's *The Light That Failed* because he had always been too busy.

☞ Douglas Adams wrote nine books before he died in 2001 but hated the process of writing. He had been promising his tenth book to his publishers for more than ten years. He died without finishing a first draft.

☞ A furious client finally managed to get her

solicitor on the phone after he had missed an important deadline. Without a good enough excuse, the solicitor panicked and pretended (very unconvincingly) to be a voicemail service.

☞ The writer E B White was often late replying to letters and came up with some imaginative excuses. He wrote to one friend, 'I would have written sooner but I got a Christmas tree ornament stuck in my pancreas, and it kept winking on and off, and I was too distracted to write letters.'

Teachers' excuses

If you think 'the dog ate my homework' is a lame excuse for being late you probably haven't heard these pathetic lines, all used by teachers ...

☞ Teachers' cats are intent on destruction. One teacher's excuse for not marking exam papers was that his cat had attacked the work. Another apologised for chewed papers, explaining that his cat had tried to eat them. And yet another teacher's cat peed on his students' coursework.

☞ A teacher in Canada apologised for returning students' exercise books late – he claimed his briefcase had been run over on the highway after it fell off the roof of his car.

☞ Students were handed back their marked test papers late, and some noticed that their papers had water marks on them. The teacher explained that his two-year-old son had peed on them and he had had to peg them on to a clothes drier and wait for them to dry out.

☞ A teacher in the US didn't return her students' exam papers. She said that she'd marked them and put them on her windowsill, then a storm had started up and blown them away. Whether or not she was telling the truth, it was true that the town had been hit by its first tornado in 30 years.

☞ University students had handed in long projects that the teacher had taken weeks to mark. At last he told the students to pick up their work from a cardboard box that would be waiting outside his room. None of the students found the box. At the next class, the professor apologised and explained that he had left the box outside his room, and the cleaners had assumed it was rubbish and thrown it away.

Quotation

'The only man who is really free is the one who can turn down an invitation to dinner without giving an excuse.'
Jules Renard

Chapter 3

The Wrong Kind of Snow:
Transport Excuses

People often blame transport for being late or not turning up. Sometimes they're telling the truth.

Transport systems are famous for coming up with excuses for bad service. If you've ever been stuck waiting for a train on an overcrowded platform in the middle of an icy downpour, you've probably heard some of them. The good thing about most of these excuses is that no one could accuse you of making them up yourself.

Rail travel

☞ 'The wrong kind of snow' has become

famous as an excuse for late-running trains. It was given in 1991 by British Rail when the train service was disrupted because of snow, even though snow had been forecast. It sounds like one of the lamest excuses ever, but the man who gave the excuse (he said 'we're having problems with the type of snow') was being perfectly reasonable: there are lots of different types of snow, and the snow that day was unusually soft and powdery, which meant it caused problems with electrical systems and yet wasn't deep enough for snow ploughs or snow blowers to be effective. It goes to show, you have to be very careful when you give an excuse, even if it's true, to make sure it doesn't sound like total nonsense.

☞ 'Leaves on the line' is another famous UK rail excuse. It sounds lamer than it is: when leaves get wet and turn to mush they cause wheels to lose traction, and wet leaves insulate electrified rails so that trains lose power. But, given the climate, and the tendency of trees to shed their leaves in the autumn, you'd have thought someone might have come up with a solution to the problem by now.

☞ When it first formed in 1948, British Rail was just as bad at excuses for late-running steam trains: passengers were told that trains between Fenchurch Street and Southend were failing because of 'the wrong kind of coal'.

☞ One wet morning a train to Bedford was cancelled 'due to slippery rain'.

☞ A London to Manchester service broke down at Rugby station, where the train's manager appealed to any passengers who had tools with them to come to the front of the train. Several people stepped forward with basic tools. One of them, straddling the front of the train trying to fix the windscreen wiper, said he'd successfully fixed the electrics on a train the week before. The passengers' efforts didn't work this time and everyone got off and used a later service.

☞ Another rail announcement told delayed passengers that the hold-up was because of 'dew on the tracks'. At least this wasn't as alarming as the reason given for a delay between St Pancras and Sheffield: 'lack of air.'

☞ 'Excessive heat on the tracks between Bedford and Luton' was the excuse for delays on the St Pancras to Derby service on the first sunny day of the year.

☞ This announcement was given at Bournemouth station: 'The train now arriving on platform one is on fire. Passengers are advised not to board this train.'
You have to admit, it's good advice.

☞ The air-conditioning system broke down on a train on a very hot July day. The excuse given was that 'the air conditioning does tend to stop working when it gets hot outside'.

☞ After hours of delays on an overcrowded train from Newcastle to London, passengers were told that the overcrowding was caused by too many passengers.

☞ A similar but ruder-sounding excuse was given on an overcrowded train in London after a match at Wembley: an announcement said that the train was delayed 'due to the weight of the passengers'.

☞ One rail announcer obviously couldn't manage a detailed excuse – he said the delay of a Thameslink train was 'due to technical technicalities'.

☞ The person making this London Underground announcement couldn't be bothered either: 'We apologise for the delay to customers on platform one. This is

Quotation

'Twenty-two minutes late, fed up by train delays, came by bike. Slow puncture at Peckham.'
Reginald Perrin, The Fall and Rise of Reginald Perrin

due to a delay in the actual service.'

☞ Passengers were surprised to hear that their train was being delayed because of Madonna. The rail company had decided to delay a service to wait for concert-goers from Wembley.

☞ Blame the Queen: trains are sometimes delayed because the royal family won't put up with delays due to level crossings – the trains are delayed instead.

☞ Delays on the line between London Fenchurch Street and Southend during rush hour were blamed on the brightness of the sun. The rail company said that a 'freak occurrence' meant that the sun was shining directly on to mirrors by the train doors, which meant that the train driver couldn't see whether passengers were getting on and off the train.

☞ Strange things sometimes end up on railway lines (see the Top Ten on page 41).

A Portakabin was found blocking the line between Watford Gap and Milton Keynes. In the US, a Union Pacific Northwest train was late because a swan was sitting on the tracks. Various other animals on the track have been blamed for delays, including horses, cows, ostriches and mating herons.

☞ An exploding pigeon was the excuse for a delay at Kings Cross Thameslink. The bird was flying between low overhead electric wires and the roof of a train and was struck by a 25,000-volt current.

☞ A sad and gruesome excuse lay behind train cancellations from Basingstoke: a cat had been electrocuted and become stuck to the driver's cab.

☞ Passengers from Inverness to London were given a series of excuses on a very, very long journey. A train was delayed by a total of five hours because of engine failure near Drumochter, faulty overhead wires at Wigan which led to a diversion, waiting for an ambulance after a passenger was taken ill at Stockport, and another diversion because of signalling equipment failure near Rugby.

Other assorted rail excuses include ...

☞ 'A drunk man on the line at Maidenhead.'

☞ 'Trespassers fighting on the line at Wilmslow.'

☞ The train driver's taxi getting lost on the way to the station.

☞ The train driver being held up in a traffic jam.

☞ The train driver having left to collect his children from school.

☞ The guard being taken away by police (he was arrested for ticket fraud).

☞ 'Trainspotters on the line.'

☞ 'A criminal under the train.'

☞ 'An escaped prisoner is threatening trains.'

☞ Flies on the windscreen (the driver had to clean the glass by hand, for some reason).

☞ A rat that had chewed through signalling cables and 'self-destructed'.

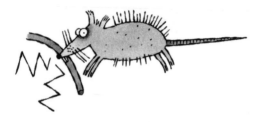

☞ 'Some idiot's used an alarm handle as a coat hook.'

☞ Most alarming of all: 'Sorry for the delay: someone is headed towards us in a car.'

Sat Nav

Satellite navigation is supposed to help car drivers get to their destinations more quickly, but sometimes it seems to have the opposite effect ...

☞ A school trip to Hampton Court Palace, where Henry VIII once lived, ended up in a narrow London alleyway after hours stuck in traffic. The driver's excuse was the sat nav: he had keyed in 'Hampton Court', expecting directions to the palace in Surrey. But instead he was directed to an alley in Islington, north London. The trip was abandoned and 60 pupils returned to their school in Hampshire eight hours after setting off, without learning anything about the Tudors.

☞ Several vehicles ended up in a metre of water because their drivers had been directed there by sat nav. A ford in the village of Luckington, Wiltshire, is often too deep for a car to cross but one satellite system was directing drivers across it anyway. People have so much faith in satellite navigation that they ignored warning signs about deep water and ended up having to be pulled out of the river by a tractor.

☞ Sat nav was the excuse for other drivers

ending up on a track impassable to most cars, with a 30-metre drop on one side, in the Yorkshire Dales. Many drivers ignored a no-through-road sign, drove through a gateway and became stuck on the narrow gravel track, near the village of Crackpot. Farmers helped pull several cars free with their tractors.

☞ Trams were delayed in Bremen, Germany, because a driver had followed sat-nav instructions and turned on to a tram line.

☞ Fans of a tribute band were disappointed to hear that the gig was cancelled a few minutes before it was due to start. The excuse was that one of the band members had mistakenly keyed 'Chelmsford' into the sat-nav system instead of 'Cheltenham'. They ended up 225 km away from where they were supposed to be playing.

☞ Two teenagers were travelling from Bournemouth to Lymington, a distance of about 30 km. Unfortunately they couldn't spell 'Lymington' and wrote down 'Limington' for their taxi driver, which he keyed into his sat-nav system. They ended up 90 km away after an hour-and-a-half drive, in a Somerset village.

Top Ten Strange but True Transport Excuses

1 Giant clown on the line

McDonalds used to use a clown, known as Ronald McDonald, as its advertising mascot. A huge inflatable Ronald McDonald had somehow broken free of its moorings and ended up on the intercity line between Cardiff and London.

2 Plague of hares confusing radar

About 80 hares were confusing the ground radar at Linate airport in Milan and a team of wildlife experts spent three hours catching them, while hundreds of people had their flights delayed. About 80 hares were finally transferred to nearby nature reserves.

⭐3 A boat on the line

A boat was blown on to the railway line between Dawlish and Teignmouth during a bad storm.

⭐4 Rat on board plane

A plane was grounded at Manila airport for 13 hours because a rat had been spotted on board. Passengers got off the plane, but after a long search the rat had still not been found and they got back on. The plane took off – with or without the rat.

⭐5 Fleas on board train

A Connex Southeast rail announcement apologised for the

cancellation of a train to Ashford, because
'the driver's cab is infested with fleas'.

6 ▶ Naked man handcuffed to luggage rack

A bridegroom-to-be
was stripped and
handcuffed to a
train's luggage rack,
then abandoned, in
an especially cruel
stag-night joke.
The Harwich-to-
London service was
delayed while firemen
released him.

7 ▶ Stowaway frogs

Passengers on a flight
from Cardiff airport
were surprised to
hear their flight was
being delayed

Quotation

'Twenty-two minutes late,
badger ate a junction box
at New Malden.'

Reginald Perrin, The Fall and Rise
of Reginald Perin

because of stow-away Cuban frogs. The tree-frogs had hopped into the cargo hold in Cuba while suitcases were being loaded for the flight to Cardiff. It took about an hour to track them down.

8 Ferret loose on train

A train was delayed because of a ferret, which had escaped its owner and alarmed passengers before getting in to the driver's cab. The animal broke into the driver's lunchbox and ate his cheese sandwiches, after which normal service was resumed.

9 'Eaves on the line'

High winds blew a roof off a house and on to railway tracks. This Southwest rail announcement was made with great delight.

10 Mushy peas on the road

Motorists stuck in an enormous traffic jam on the A1 road near Grantham were told by police that the reason for the delay was

the road being covered in peas. A lorry
shed 18 tonnes of them after a collision
with a bus. No one was seriously hurt but
millions of peas were completely crushed.

Air travel

You've probably been stuck in an airport (or, worse,
stuck in a cramped plane) facing hours of delay,
while you should have been relaxing on your
holiday. Flights are often delayed and the most
common excuses involve air traffic control,
equipment failure, inbound flights arriving late
and bad weather. But some are a bit more
interesting ...

☞ Passengers were stranded for 11 hours at
Bournemouth airport, after their plane set off
for Portugal then turned back an hour into
the flight. Apparently the plane had flown
into a huge swarm of bees, which had
affected the engines.

☞ A flight from Tel Aviv was delayed for several

hours while a bird-catcher was called in to remove a tiny bird from the cockpit of a plane.

☞ Passengers on a flight from Tenerife to Cardiff were told there would be a delay in landing because an air traffic controller was on a tea break.

☞ A flight from Boston, USA, was delayed while a passenger was arrested for carrying a seal's head with him in a canvas cooler. The man claimed to be a university professor and said he was going to use the head for educational purposes.

☞ A flight was delayed in 2004 when Paris Hilton tried to get on board with a goat, a monkey and a ferret she'd just bought. She took the animals home by limo instead.

☞ Sometimes planes are delayed because of cats and dogs on the loose at airports. A stray dog at the airport in Phoenix, Arizona, was chased for hours until it was finally caught in the baggage garage.

☞ A technical problem with a plane caused flight delays and cancellations. The Nepali airline who owned it sacrificed two goats to Akash Bhairab, the Hindu god of sky protection, after which it reported that the aircraft made a successful flight to Hong Kong.

☞ Two pilots were taxiing an Arizona-bound flight to the runway at Miami, Florida, when they were stopped and taken off the plane because they were still drunk from a drinking session the night before. They were later prosecuted.

☞ A flight from Berlin to London was delayed because of snow. A few passengers were allowed to leave but most had to sit on the plane for 7.5 hours. Six of them started criminal proceedings against the pilot, claiming 'false imprisonment'.

Funny Feet

These are five of the best reasons given for needing transport to a health clinic:

'I can't breathe and haven't done so for years.'

'I hope you will still send your driver, as my husband is quite useless.'

'I can't walk any distance because I have a hip.'

'I must have transport as I have funny feet.'

'My husband is dead and will not bring me.'

Chapter 4

Doh! Excuses for Doing Stupid Things

We all do stupid things from time to time. Maybe you've forgotten the bath was running or left your keys in the front door. But how about putting a live rattlesnake inside your mouth? Or shooting a hole in your car? These and many other foolish actions all have their excuses ...

☞ Eleven teenagers in Northern Ireland jumped from a cliff and were swept out to sea. Seven managed to swim ashore and four others had to be rescued by lifeboat. Their excuse was that they'd been making a film about the stupid risks taken by students.

☞ A Florida man shot a hole in the exhaust pipe of his car and, perhaps not surprisingly, was hit in the leg by pieces of bullet and shrapnel and ended up in hospital. His excuse was that he was repairing the car, needed to make a hole in the exhaust and couldn't find a drill. So, obviously ...

☞ One man actually shot himself in the shoulder with a rifle 'to see how it felt'. The following year he did it again because 'it felt so good'.

☞ A British soldier back from duty in Iraq ended up in hospital after he stuck a firework between his buttocks and set light to it. He said he'd been bored with the firework display he was watching.

☞ A police chief from Ohio, USA, made a stupid mistake and came up with an

elaborate and even
more stupid excuse for
it. Somehow, he had
managed to fire his
rifle through the
windscreen of his
police car. To cover up the accident the
police chief radioed his station with a story
that he'd pulled over a car with no license
plates and the driver had opened fire. To add
realistic sound effects, he fired his gun, then
accidentally fired it again, shooting himself in
the leg. A search was launched for a tall,
bearded man responsible for wounding the
police chief. A week later, the chief confessed
that he'd made up the whole story.

Quotation
'Nobody likes to offer
stupidity as an excuse.'
Mason Cooley

☞ A foolish collector of snakes captured a huge
rattlesnake on the road in Oregon, USA. A
few weeks later he got out the snake at a
barbeque and waved it dangerously close to
his girlfriend. When she protested, he said,
'It's a nice snake. Nothing can happen.
Watch!' and put the snake's head in his

mouth. It bit him on the tongue. After a lot of pain, a tracheotomy and several days in hospital, the man regained consciousness. His only excuse was that he'd been drunk ... and stupid.

☞ Another man nearly died after he was bitten on the lip by a rattlesnake when he'd tried to kiss it. He'd done it for a dare.

☞ Stupid people and snakes are a very bad combination. A hiker in Scotland picked up two snakes so that his brother could take a photo. One was a grass snake but the other was a black adder, Britain's only venomous snake. Both creatures bit him and he had to be hospitalised. His excuse was that he hadn't realised there were any venomous snakes in Scotland.

☞ Singer Michael Jackson dangled his nine-month-old baby over a hotel balcony four storeys high. Ironically, he was in Berlin to accept an award for his work with children. His only excuse was that he 'got caught up in the excitement of the moment'.

☞ A Romanian man told police that he had murdered someone and wanted to give himself up because he had run out of money and needed to get home. Police soon discovered that he had made up the crime, but the man was fined and asked to cover expenses for being driven 160 km to his home.

☞ A toilet museum in the Ukraine has had to put notices on its exhibits telling the public not to use them after a visitor made use of one of them. The man apologised and explained that he hadn't realised the toilets were only to look at.

☞ A Swiss club owner set fire to his own club

and burned it to the ground. He was trying to demonstrate to safety inspectors that the building was fire-proof by setting fire to paper ornaments.

☞ A German man tried to climb into a friend's flat in the early hours of the morning and ended up getting stuck in a chimney. His cries for help were eventually heard – 12 hours later – by a cleaner. He was rescued by the fire brigade, who had to knock a hole in the chimney to release him, and taken to hospital where he soon recovered. His excuse: he'd been drinking at the Munich Oktoberfest beer festival.

☞ You know how it is: you've had a few beers, you climb down a chimney ... A man from Indiana, USA, climbed down his ex-girlfriend's chimney in the middle of the night and became stuck. He had to be rescued by firefighters. His excuse: 'we all do stupid things when we're drunk.' His girlfriend thought he should have been left in the chimney.

☞ Being extremely drunk was also the excuse of a man who robbed a bank masked in his own underpants and ran away with the money. Unfortunately for him, his demand note had his wife's name on the other side of the paper and police soon tracked him down. The man said he didn't remember the robbery because he'd been so drunk, but had become suspicious the next morning when he saw a photo of the robber in the paper wearing a pair of pants that looked familiar, and found a huge wad of cash in his pocket.

☞ A Los Angeles man made aviation history when he decided to take a flight in his garden chair. He attached 45 helium-filled weather balloons to his comfy chair, packed some sandwiches and beer and signalled for a friend to cut the rope that attached him to his car. But instead of rising gently upwards and hovering above his garden, as he'd planned, the man was immediately whisked into the sky to a height of 16,000 feet. Cold and terrified, the man was too afraid to shoot the balloons with the pellet gun he'd brought along for the purpose, in case it unbalanced the chair and tipped him out. The man crossed the flight path into LAX airport and various pilots made reports of the strange sight. After a 14-hour flight, he finally summoned the courage to shoot some of the balloons and descended, where he became entangled in power cables and cut off electricity to a district of LA for 20 minutes. He managed to climb safely down to earth and was immediately arrested. When asked for a reason for his idiotic stunt, he replied, 'A man can't just sit around.'

Quotation
'One year ago today, the time for excuse-making has come to an end.
George W Bush

☞ A man burned his own house down when he

set fire to a pile of his underpants in his back garden because he couldn't find a clean pair and became furious. Luckily, no one was hurt in the fire but the damage was estimated at £60,000.

☞ A Canadian man tried to eat his own underwear. He'd been pulled over by police for driving erratically, and was trying to absorb the alcohol he'd drunk before he took a breathalyzer test.

☞ A pigeon was the unlikely excuse for a huge punch-up between neighbouring families in Melbourne, Australia. The neighbours got into an argument about who owned the pigeon and were soon fighting. Five people ended up in hospital.

☞ A man from Los Angeles stole a steamroller with a top speed of 8 km per hour. He was soon captured by police. He said he had been 'tired of walking'.

☞ A robber was trying to hold-up a shop but

didn't get very far before security guards arrived. He pretended to be just an ordinary shopper ... but he'd forgotten that he was still wearing a pair of tights over his head.

☞ A student from Ohio stuck his head close to a moving train and, luckily, only suffered cuts and bruises. He told police he'd been trying to find out how close he could get to the train without getting hit.

Quotation
'He that is good for making excuses is seldom good for anything else.'
Benjamin Franklin

Chapter 5
Time Off

Sometimes, taking time off school, college or work is unavoidable for a very good reason: storms, floods, rampaging moose, family crises. And sometimes people just can't be bothered to turn up – and who can blame them? – so they invent an excuse that they hope sounds plausible.

Missing school

☞ Four students at Duke University in the US were having such a good time while they were away for the weekend that they decided to stay for Sunday night, even though they had a final exam on Monday. They came up with an excuse: they told their professor that they'd been on their way back from a weekend break when they got a flat tyre. They'd had to wait a long time for help and made it back to university too late to sit the exam. The professor agreed that they could sit the exam the following day instead and the students were relieved. The next day, each student was given the exam paper in a separate room. The first question looked straightforward enough and was worth five points. But they got a shock when they turned over the page and looked at the second question: 'For 95 points: which tyre?'

☞ Back in 1999 some people were afraid that the year 2000 would cause all sorts of terrible problems because of the way computer date systems were set up. Computer systems that controlled electricity, gas and government services could all be thrown into chaos, they believed. One parent sent in an unusual excuse note for her son: he would be missing a week of school because the whole family were attending a millennium survival workshop – 'just in case'.

☞ University students arrived at their first class of the day to find it had been cancelled. Their professor explained that there was a bat flying around the classroom. Apparently, the animal had been noticed in the room before, but it had just hung there not bothering anybody.

☞ One student didn't come into college on 14 February. He explained that he hadn't turned up because 'Valentine's Day is so commercial'.

☞ During the spring, a girl in Alaska sometimes had an unusual excuse for missing school: a dangerous moose. The female moose would occasionally spend time in front of her house with its calf. No one could go in or out of the house because moose can become very fierce when they have young to protect.

☞ A naughty pupil hadn't revised for an important mock exam one morning, so she didn't go. She went into school at lunchtime with an excuse she knew her squeamish teacher wouldn't follow up: she told her in a very loud whisper, 'I had diarrhoea.' It worked.

☞ After nearly a whole term of a 16-year-old student arriving late or not turning up at all, an art teacher had a serious talk with him. The boy explained that his grandmother was in intensive care, and that this had triggered a recurrence of his Obsessive–Compulsive Disorder, which meant he felt compelled to wash himself and clean things repeatedly, which often delayed him leaving home. The compassionate

Quotation

'Ninety-nine percent of the failures come from people who have the habit of making excuses.'
George Washington Carver

teacher was full of sympathy and immediately sent an email to other staff members, asking them to make allowances for the student. He also sent a letter to the boy's parents. He was shocked to receive a reply from them, telling him that there was no grandmother in intensive care, and no OCD either.

Top Ten School Excuse Notes

The following are from excuse notes handed in to teachers in Britain and the US. Some are funny, some are strange and most have absolutely terrible spelling.

1 Please excuse Jason for being absent yesterday. He had a cold and could not breed well.

2 Please excuse Jennifer for missing school yesterday. We forgot to get the Sunday paper off the porch, and when we found it on Monday, we thought it was Sunday.

3 Please excuse Jason from school today as he has misplaced his trousers.

4 Ralph was absent yesterday because of a sour trout.

(Maybe a sore throat, or maybe a case of food poisoning?)

5 My son is under a doctor's care and should not take PE today. Please execute him.

6 Please excuse Lisa for being absent. She was sick and I had her shot.

7 Please ekscuse John being absent on Jan. 28, 29, 30, 31, 32, and also 33.

8 Please excuse Roland from PE for a few days. Yesterday he fell out of a tree and misplaced his hip.

9 Please excuse Tommy for being absent yesterday. He had diarrhoea and his boots leak.

> *Quotation*
>
> 'Life is full of excuses to feel pain, excuses not to live, excuses, excuses, excuses.'
>
> *Erica Jong*

Frank's leg is hurting real bad. From Mum.

(This one didn't work.)

Missing work

It's amazing how often domestic crises strike – burst pipes, leaking washing machines, cars that won't start – all of which can mean being forced to take time off work. Here are a few more imaginative excuses:

☞ A young Peruvian financial analyst began work at a New York company. After a few weeks, he called his boss to say he'd been called up to the Peruvian Army, so he needed a day off to find out what to do about it. The following day, he needed time off to plead his case with the Peruvian Ambassador. Then even worse news arrived: the young man would need to go to Peru to try and get out of his army service. His boss granted him a few more days off. Then his mother phoned with the news that her son was still in Peru, still trying to negotiate with the army. The same day, a colleague ran into the young man on the subway. It turned out that he'd been working for a rival company.

☞ A woman in Gloucestershire was surprised when her driving instructor didn't turn up for her lesson but she later found out that he had a good and very unusual excuse: he'd gone to give a driving lesson to a monk and walked underneath another monk cleaning the guttering, who fell off his ladder and squashed him.

☞ Inventing a bereavement is a common way of skiving off work. One office worker was caught out when he called and told his boss that his granny had died – the boss had kept records and replied that this was the employee's fourth dead grandmother.

☞ A distraught marketing executive said that he wouldn't be in that day because his favourite *American Idol* contestant had been voted off and he'd been up all night.

☞ An estate agent called his office and explained that he'd need some time off while he waited for a friend of his to turn up with some clothes: during the night his girlfriend had chopped up every item of clothing he owned with a pair of shears. He didn't offer to explain why.

☞ A woman on a skiing trip decided to call work and say that there'd been a blizzard and the flight was delayed, so she would have to catch a flight the following day and miss a day's work. The next morning there really was a blizzard and she was snowed in for four days.

☞ A shop assistant failed to turn up for work one day and didn't

Quotation

'We are all manufacturers – some make good, others make trouble, and still others make excuses.'

H V Adolt

call in sick. The following day she came in at the usual time, in tears, and told her manager that she'd spent the whole of the day before at a police station making a statement about her daughter's father. She claimed he had become violent and threatened her and her child. All of the woman's colleagues were sympathetic and understanding. But a few weeks later they found out the truth: she hadn't spent the day at a police station but on a mini-break to Barcelona, she hadn't been threatened by anyone, and in fact she didn't even have a child.

☞ A superstitious personal assistant explained that she wouldn't be in work that day because her psychic had warned her to stay at home, otherwise something terrible would certainly happen to her.

Top Ten Strange Excuses for Missing Work

Bosses around the world received these excuses for

time off work with raised eyebrows ...

1 'My dog swallowed my bus pass.'

2 'I was poisoned by my mother-in-law.'

3 'I was arrested as a result of mistaken identity.'

4 'I accidentally drove through the automatic garage door before it opened.'

5 'A buffalo escaped from the game reserve and kept charging me every time I tried to go to my car from my house.'

6 'My horses got loose and are running down the highway.'

> ## Quotation
> 'You heard me, I won't be in for the rest of the week. I told you, my baby beat me up. Oh, it's not the worst excuse I ever thought up.'
> Homer Simpson, The Simpsons

7 'I accidentally flushed my car keys down the toilet.'

8 'I was sprayed by a skunk.'

9 'My monkey died.'

10 'I had to deliver my sister's baby and need time to recover.'

Sickies

Some people manage to
keep their job despite
rarely working a full week
– in fact the only time
they seem to be in perfect
health is when they're on
holiday.

Quotation
'The person who really
wants to do something
finds a way; the other
person finds an excuse.'
Anonymous

☞ Continual colds, bouts of '24-hour flu', upset
stomachs etc. accounted for ten sick days in
the first six months of one young woman
starting a new job in an IT company. Her
boss finally had enough when the employee's
excuse for a single day off was 'toxic shock
syndrome', an extremely rare and very
dangerous form of blood poisoning.

☞ Never forge a sick note if you're a bit hazy
about biology. A South African man faked a
note from the gynaecologist his pregnant
girlfriend was seeing, not realising that only
women consult gynaecologists.

☞ One man called in sick at 9am. Two hours later his boss found that he needed to ask him a question and phoned his home number. The man's wife answered, saying, 'He's out playing golf all morning, try his mobile.'

☞ Two workers at a Scottish company both asked for the day off to watch a World Cup football match. They were turned down. Their boss became suspicious when both workers called in sick on the day of the match and hired a private detective agency. The pair were filmed leaving their homes and going to a pub to watch the match.

☞ A young stage manager at a London theatre called in to say she had gastric flu and was off work for a couple of days. Unfortunately for her, she wasn't very good at keeping her

Quotation
'The comfort zone takes our greatest aspirations and turns them into excuses for not bothering to aspire.'
Peter McWilliams

head down: on the
second day her boss
caught her in the local
burger bar scoffing
onion rings.

Quotation

'The real man is one w
always finds excuses fo
others, but never excuse
himself.'
Henry Ward Beecher

☞ An office worker in
Florida called his boss at
about 11am to say that he had just had
surgery on his hemorrhoids and wouldn't be
able to come to work for the rest of the day.
The boss asked why he hadn't known about
the surgery in advance and was told that it
was 'emergency surgery'. The next day the
man arrived with an inflatable doughnut-
shaped cushion to sit on. The boss believed
him.

TOP 10 **Top Ten Sick of Work Excuses**

1 *'I broke my leg snowboarding off my roof while drunk.'*

2 *'I was walking down the street watching road*

works being done, fell in the hole and hurt myself.'

3 'I have a bad case of the hiccups.'

4 'I tasted some dog food because the dog was not feeling well, and now I'm sick.'

5 'I was bitten by a camel on a trip to the zoo.'

6 'I blew my nose so hard, my back went out.'

7 'At my sister's wedding I chipped my tooth on a Mint Julep, bent over to spit it out, hit my head on a keg and was knocked unconscious with a mild concussion.'

8 'I have head lice.'

9 'I tripped over my dog and was knocked unconscious.'

10 'I was injured while getting a haircut.'

Slacking at work

You can be physically present at work or school and still take time off. It's known as slacking. Slacking can take various forms, from internet time-wasting to long lunch hours and out-of-office 'meetings' – and slackers are always ready with an excuse.

- Daydreaming at school or work is something everyone does from time to time. If you're sitting quietly at your desk 'working' or 'studying' you won't need an excuse because no one will notice anyway. But if you're in the middle of a meeting or lesson where you might well be asked a question, it's a bad idea to drift off. If you have a tendency to do this, try to come up with a general purpose comment beforehand. If the worst happens and you are forced to admit that you have no idea what was being said, your excuse could

Quotation

'Sometimes I wish I had a terrible childhood so that at least I'd have an excuse.'
Jimmy Fallon

be that you were mentally grappling with some relevant problem and didn't hear the last couple of minutes: maybe a difficult equation, or working out an average for some complicated aspect of your work.

• Actually nodding off is less easy to get out of. Even if you are screened from other people, you can't guarantee that someone won't discover you sleeping at your desk. Possible excuses include:

'I gave blood at lunchtime.'

'I took a cold remedy to keep me going through this flu – it must have knocked me out.'

'I was up all night working on those figures.'

One office worker, disturbed from a nap, thought quickly and said, '…Amen.'

• IT managers estimate the average amount of time spent on 'social networking' websites like MySpace and Facebook while at work is about 50 minutes every day. Here are some excuses you might like to try if you're ever caught looking at irrelevant websites on work or school time ...

☞ *'This website is incredibly popular – I'm trying to figure out their marketing strategy.'*

☞ *'It's research.'*

☞ *'I found this site in this PC's web history and I thought it might be relevant – but, as you can see, far from it!'*

☞ *'These pop-ups are so annoying.'*

☞ *'Did you know viruses can change all your bookmarks?'*

Quotation
'No one ever excused his way to success.'
Dave Del Dotto

☞ *'Tut! Who keeps sending these stupid links?'*

☞ *'Have you noticed how many irrelevant links there are in genuine news articles?'*

☞ *'Honestly! Isn't there a firewall to stop this kind of rubbish getting through?'*

- One company discovered that an employee was spending six hours every day acting as a moderator for a social networking site when he was supposed to be working. Not surprisingly, the employee couldn't think of a good enough excuse and got the sack.

> ## Quotation
> 'Whoever wants to be a judge of human nature should study people's excuses.'
> *Christian Friedrich Hebbel*

Slacking when you're supposed to be working at home

Students everywhere, and anyone with a job that allows them to work from home, will know that just about anything, even cleaning the cooker, is more appealing than doing any work. The situation is made worse by the fact that the only person you have to make an excuse to is yourself. Here's a list of handy excuses you might like to use to convince yourself not to do any work:

☞ You can't work in a pigsty.

Housework in all its forms becomes strangely appealing. You might find it necessary to do a thorough spring clean before starting any work.

☞ You need to keep your strength up.

Now might be the time to try out that complicated recipe you saw on telly the other night. It's brain food.

☞ It's unhealthy to sit at a desk all day.

Regular exercise is essential, especially if you need to burn off some extra calories from the 'brain food'. Getting out for a good, long power walk might be a good idea.

☞ It's important not to become isolated.

You'll need to stay in touch with colleagues and/or students, of course. And keeping in touch with friends is necessary to your general wellbeing.

☞ You need regular breaks.

It's a legal requirement to have a ten-minute
break from staring at a computer screen
every hour. Or something like that. You run
the risk of RSI if you don't take regular rests
from typing, too. Besides, an hour or two for
lunch while you think about other things
will make you better able to concentrate in
the afternoon.

While working on this book I've taken five three-
hour lunch breaks (owing to pressures of work), had
several afternoons off (RSI), taken several two-day
breaks (family crises), a week off with a bad back, an
awful lot of tea breaks (eye strain), a ten-day holiday
in Malta (after a particularly stressful few weeks),
made six carrot cakes (to cheer up myself or
depressed family members), and spent a total of 36
hours on the phone. I've also spring-cleaned the
house six times and done a *lot* of ironing. The book
was originally due to be published in 2005.

LEAVE
ON THE
LINE

If you need to give yourself a good excuse for taking a whole day off, here are a few ideas ...

☞ Darwin Day, on 12 February, celebrates the birth of Charles Darwin – if you're a scientist it's your duty to take the day off to remember the great man. Or you could suggest this to your biology teacher. (Also remember 24 November – that was the date in 1859 that Darwin's *Origin of the Species* was first published.)

☞ If you're a system administrator you absolutely must have a holiday on the last Friday of July for System Administrator Appreciation Day (www.sysadminday.com). If you're not a system administrator, why not start a holiday for people who work in your industry or study your subject?

☞ Maths students and teachers,

Quotation

'And oftentimes excusing of a fault Doth make the fault the worse by the excuse.'
William Shakespeare

accountants and everyone else who likes sums should all celebrate pi day on 14 March. (3.14, as Americans might write the date, is a very rough pi equivalent.)

☞ Useful dates for English students and teachers, or anyone involved in publishing, include 23 April (William Shakespeare's birthday – probably), 16 December (Jane Austen's birthday), and 7 February (Charles Dickens's birthday). Whatever your line of study or work, you will find that you should take the day off in honour of someone famous – or perhaps several people.

☞ Then there are national holidays, cultural festivals, strange regional events like Cheese Rolling, and silly festivals like No Pants Day (the first Friday in May if you're interested but, be warned, these are American pants, i.e. *trousers*). Give it some thought and you should be able to find an excuse for at least one day off a month.

Chapter 6

It's Not You, It's Me: Dating Excuses

You know how it is – once, you found him incredibly attractive, hilariously funny and sharply intelligent. Now, every time he opens his mouth you want to strangle him. But no one wants to hurt another person's feelings, especially when that person wants to hold your hand and call you Bunnikins. What can you do?

☞ A Scottish woman took her boyfriend out for a last romantic meal, where she broke the

news: 'I love you, but I'm being sent out of the country on a top secret mission and I won't be able to see you for the next five to seven years.' Devasted, the couple parted – then bumped into each other a few weeks later in a shopping centre in a nearby city.

☞ In a similar situation, a US couple had been together for about a year. From the start, the guy had claimed he was a federal agent who couldn't talk about his job, and he never revealed much about his life or friends either. One day, he left a phone message cancelling their date that evening, then never got in touch again. At first, the girl couldn't work out why he wasn't returning her calls, then she started to imagine that something terrible had happened. But it wasn't long before she had news of him – he'd been arrested for fraud in an internet scam. He'd made up everything he'd said about his FBI job.

☞ Being stood up is a particularly cruel way of finding out you've been dumped. One girl had a great time on a first date and confidently waited in a coffee shop to see the boy again. When he didn't turn up and didn't reply to her texts and phone messages, she was convinced something must have happened to him and called the police, who quickly found out that she'd been stood up.

☞ Henry VIII had six wives and needed good excuses for getting out of four of his marriages. Henry managed to get the marriage to his first wife annulled because she'd been married to his brother (who died) before she married Henry (which hadn't seemed to matter for most of their 24-year marriage). Henry invented evidence of unfaithfulness and witchcraft for his second wife. Henry wasn't keen on his fourth wife's looks and said he'd been misled by a portrait, and his fifth wife was also accused of being unfaithful.

Quotation
'Two wrongs don't m. a right, but they make good excuse.'
Thomas Szasz

☞ US novelist Henry Miller used an imaginative excuse for breaking up with his wife after he'd been unfaithful to her and she'd caught him out. He said, 'I

Quotation

'I've heard 'em all: "I like you as a friend", "I think we should see other people", "I no speak English", "I'm married to the sea", "I don't want to kill you, but I will ..."

Homer Simpson, The Simpsons

couldn't tolerate being married to a woman who didn't trust me.'

☞ Sometimes what sounds like a lame excuse is actually the truth. A girl made no reply when her boyfriend texted her with an especially slushy message. They bumped into one another the next day and he was so hurt that he blanked her. In fact she'd dropped her phone down the loo (one of the most common excuses given to insurers of mobiles, by the way) but it took a week of sulking before he believed her story.

IT WASN'T MY FAULT ...

Top Ten Most Common Dating Excuses

If you've ever been dumped, the chances are that you heard something like at least one of the following lines:

1 There's too much going on in my life at the moment.

2 I'm confused and need some time apart.

3 I love you but I'm not in love with you.

4 I need more freedom/space (often followed by, 'perhaps we should stay together but see other people too?').

5 I'm still not over my previous relationship.

6 I'm not good enough for you. You deserve better than me.

7 I guess I'm just not ready to commit.

8 It's not you, it's me.

9 I'm not ready for a relationship.

We have something special, it's just the wrong time for me.

Among the lines you definitely wouldn't want to hear:

☞ I'm marrying someone else.

☞ I'm in love with your best friend.

☞ My husband/wife has found out about us.

☞ I've been seeing the same girl your last boyfriend cheated on you with.

All have been delivered to unfortunate victims.

Some people can't stand the idea of dumping someone face to face, so they phone, email or – the ultimate insult – text. If you've received a 'ur dumped' message you are in good company: Britney Spears dumped her husband Kevin Federline by text, and the Prime Minister of Finland used SMS to dump his girlfriend.

And some people can't even face the thought of

sending a text. So instead they don't get in touch again and never answer the phone. Maybe these people are just so sensitive that they can't bear to see another person in pain ... or maybe they're just callous pigs. Either way, this method of dumping someone has become an awful lot easier since caller ID.

Quotation

'Look, Fry, you're a m and I'm a woman. We' just too different.'
Leela, Futurama

Maybe you've been on the receiving end of an insulting dumping excuse. If you have, you could seek support at www.soyouvebeendumped.com – a website for dumpees. Here are some of the real break-up lines collected by the website. It seems not everyone looks for a kind way to tell someone it's over:

'I have no empathy for you, just contempt, and I think about suicide rather than staying with you.'

'I would rather live in my car and be a drug addict than spend another moment with you.'

'Yes, I love you, but I really, really hate you too.'

'You talked about the future, and that freaked me out.
It makes me sick to think about it.'

And these dumpers did find excuses – but really,
really lame ones:

'We have too many music differences. I really like the
new Radiohead stuff and you're just into the old stuff.'

'You just know me too well, and that freaks me out.
You know what I am going to do before I do it, so I
can't do anything.'

'Ever since we started dating, I just don't have the time
to do the things that are important to me. I love you,
but I want to spend more time golfing and painting.'

Wedding bells

☞ A Norwegian woman charged with bigamy
came up with a rather lame excuse: she said
she had forgotten she was already married.

Admittedly it was her fourth marriage in two years, so maybe it really did slip her mind ... then again, her husband was only on holiday when she married someone else. Not many people's memories are *that* bad.

☞ A Guatemalan man couldn't bear to tell his fiancée that he didn't want to go through with the wedding. On the wedding day, the man disappeared. He reappeared hours later, claiming that he'd been kidnapped, and gave a statement to the police. But the police soon discovered that the man was lying and had run away simply to avoid getting married. He was charged with wasting police time.

☞ A London man didn't turn up for his wedding, got his best man to make his excuses for him, and went off on the couple's honeymoon to Tahiti on his own. The bride-to-be bravely went ahead with the huge wedding

Quotation

'Love will find a way. Indifference will find an excuse.'
Anonymous

reception they'd planned. She later learned that her ex-fiancé had jilted someone else on her wedding day a few years before.

☞ A Welsh policeman used 'family illness' as his excuse to cancel his wedding to a fellow police officer on the day of their wedding. The real reason was that he was already married to someone else.

Sometimes it's just inexcusable ...

☞ A Romanian man had a wife and a girlfriend and bought them each a surprise present: necklaces engraved with their initials and a special message on each one. Unfortunately for him, he mixed up the gifts and both women got more of a surprise than he'd bargained for. His wife started divorce proceedings the same day.

☞ A young man was living
with his girlfriend in
England when he met an
American woman and
decided he wanted to be
with her. He prepared for
a new life in America but
couldn't quite bring himself to tell his
girlfriend the truth, so he told her he'd found
a new job in America and would be leaving
without her. Then he changed his mind ...
sort of. He said he'd still have to take the job,
but only for a few weeks. He was found out
in the end, when the two women ended up
talking on the phone he'd left behind in
America while he was on his way back to
England. He had a surprise waiting for him
at the airport ...

Quotation

'The absent are never
without fault, nor the
present without
excuse.'
Benjamin Franklin

☞ A two-timing Londoner was given away by
his parrot. His girlfriends both became
suspicious when it kept repeating, 'Hello, Julie,'
to Helen, and, 'Give us a kiss, Helen,' to Julie.

☞ A football referee at an amateur match in Brazil went to pull a red card out of his pocket but instead produced a pair of red, frilly, women's knickers. He was very embarrassed, especially since the knickers didn't belong to his wife, who was watching the match and filed for divorce straight afterwards.

Chapter 7

Ooops – Excuses for Accidents and Mistakes

What would you do if you were responsible for blowing the roof off your parents' house? Would you grovel and offer to work as a slave for your mum and dad for the rest of your life, or blame the dog? The thought of facing up to the consequences might make you try to shirk responsibility ...

Anyone Can Make a Mistake ...

☞ Surgeons in China operated on a young boy to correct a limp but they made an important error: they lengthened the wrong leg. The chief doctor's excuse was that when the boy was anaesthetised he was lying on his back, but when the surgery was performed he had been turned over on to his stomach.

☞ A museum visitor accidentally smashed three valuable 17th Century Chinese vases into hundreds of pieces. A specialist ceramics restorer took two and a half days to glue just one of the vases back together at the Fitzwilliam Museum in Cambridge. The man responsible for the breakage was arrested but released without charge, although the museum wouldn't let him back inside. He explained that he'd tripped over his own shoelaces.

☞ A grandfather called Brian was sent a letter asking him to attend the maternity unit at Nottingham City Hospital for a scan of his unborn baby. The hospital admitted that there had been an error, which it said was due to 'training a new member of staff'.

☞ 'I forgot' isn't much of an excuse – especially when it's the only one you can come up with for leaving your baby in the back of a cab. A Romanian woman got out of a cab at a bingo hall and paid the driver. Later the cabbie investigated noises in the back of his taxi, discovered a baby in it and drove back to the bingo hall.

☞ As Vice President of the United States, Dan Quayle attended a spelling bee at a school in New Jersey where he asked a student to spell the word 'potato'. The 12-year-old boy spelled the word correctly, but Quayle told him to add an 'e', spelling 'potatoe'. His excuse was that the school had provided 'incorrect written material'.

Quotation

'Never ruin an apology with an excuse.'
Kimberly Johnson

Dan Quayle became famous for slips of the tongue, and plain nonsense, including:

☞ 'Welcome President Bush, Mrs Bush and my fellow astronauts.'

☞ 'It's time for the human race to enter the solar system.'

☞ 'If we don't succeed, we run the risk of failure.'

☞ 'What a waste it is to lose one's mind. Or not to have a mind is being very wasteful. How true that is.'

☞ 'I stand by all the misstatements that I've made.'

☞ 'The American people would not want to know of any misquotes that Dan Quayle may or may not make.'

☞ In his autobiography, Quayle said that the media's 'obsession with my small verbal blunders went beyond the bounds of fairness'.

☞ US President Andrew Jackson's spelling was once criticised. He replied that it was 'an unimaginative man who could not spell a word more than one way'.

☞ Homework can be dangerous: a chemistry student blew up his dormitory at the Moscow State University. His excuse was that he'd been mixing chemicals as part of his homework.

☞ An 18-year-old stayed at home while his parents went on holiday. Imagine their surprise when they returned to find that the roof had been blown off the family house. The teenager had put a washing basket on top of the electric cooker, then he must have accidentally turned on one of the rings before he went out. The clothes in the washing basket caught fire and set light to a bag of shopping containing a can of deodorant, which exploded, blowing the roof off. All together there was about £35,000's worth of damage to the house. When the boy told his parents about it, he blamed the family dog – he said it must have jumped up on to the kitchen counter. Hmmm.

☞ 'I was very tired and not thinking straight,' said a man who filled his car with petrol in central Italy then drove for six hours all the way to Germany before he noticed that he'd left something behind at the petrol station: his wife.

☞ In 1987 an extremely severe storm, with record-breaking high winds, caused terrible damage in southern England. The evening before, weather presenter Michael Fish told the nation in his weather report: 'Earlier on today apparently a lady rang the BBC and said she heard that there was a hurricane on the way. Well don't worry if you're watching, there isn't.'

Mr Fish claims that he wasn't talking about the UK when he made the remark, but the Caribbean. But whether his excuse is genuine or not, he's been remembered for the mistake for more than 20 years.

☞ Anglia TV played the wrong tape and broadcast a weather report full of swear words as the presenter stumbled over her script. The TV company blamed 'technical problems'.

☞ Talking about a complaint received from a Lancashire man about a large gas bill, a spokesman for North West Gas said, 'We agree it was rather high for the time of year. It's possible Mr Purdey has been charged for the gas used up during the explosion that destroyed his house.'

We all hope that Mr Purdey has his bill reduced.

☞ A catfish called Kipper was given the blame for a house fire in Dorset. Water splashed from the aquarium on to an electric plug, which caused the fire. A smoke alarm saved the family, but sadly the guilty fish died.

☞ When Janet Jackson revealed one of her boobs on national television in a duet with Justin Timberlake, Timberlake demonstrated the fine art of excuse-making when he explained that it was a 'wardrobe malfunction'.

☞ The excuse given for the sinking of the Titanic, which killed thousands of people when it hit an iceberg in the Atlantic in 1912, was that the sea was too calm – an excuse made by the look-out and the captain.

It sounds lame but in fact it's a reasonable excuse – in rougher seas it's easier to spot icebergs because of the waves breaking against them. Which goes to show, sometimes it's better not to say anything at all.

☞ Mid and South Wales Safety Camera
Partnership apologised after they accused a
taxi driver of driving his 12-year-old Vauxhall
Cavalier at 420mph. They blamed an
'employee processing error'.

☞ A Mars orbiter worth
$125 million went
missing because the
company that built
and operated the
orbiter for NASA
provided navigation
commands in feet and
inches while NASA used metric units. The
mistake meant that the orbiter was thrown
out of orbit and was last seen in 1999
heading for the Sun. The chief administrator
of the project didn't put the blame on
individuals but NASA's 'systems engineering'.

☞ If you've ever sent a text message and then
really, really wished you hadn't, you might
consider the following story as a possible

excuse. A Welsh man realised that he was sleep-texting – sending text messages while asleep. His friend received a message from him that asked for help because someone was chasing him. Alarmed, the friend phoned him back straight away to find that the night-time texter was just having a nightmare. Other texts sent by the man while asleep in the middle of the night include one about a film he'd seen that day and various messages to his mum.

So, maybe the embarrassing text was your unconscious mind. It's worth a try.

☞ Christopher Columbus sailed to the West Indies in 1492 but his calculations had convinced him he should be in India – which is quite a long way away. So he theorised that the world wasn't round at all, but pear-shaped.

Quotation
'Justifying a fault doubles it.'
Proverb

Car accidents

If you travel by road, you'll know that there are a lot of dangerous idiots out there (of course, you aren't one of them) and if there's any kind of accident it is *always* caused by one of the dangerous idiots. Or possibly an invisible car, a telephone pole or the road doing something unexpected. These are quotes from motor insurance claims forms ...

☞ *'The accident happened because I had one eye on the lorry in front, one eye on the pedestrian and the other on the car behind.'*

☞ *'I started to slow down but the traffic was more stationary than I thought.'*

☞ *'Going to work at 7am this morning I drove out of my drive straight into a bus. The bus was five minutes early.'*

☞ *'I started to turn and it was at this point I noticed a camel and an elephant tethered at the verge. This distraction caused me to lose concentration and hit a bollard.'*

☞ *'The other car collided with mine without giving warning of its intention.'*

☞ *'I collided with a stationary truck coming the other way.'*

☞ *'A pedestrian hit me and went under my car.'*

☞ *'I had been shopping for plants all day and was on my way home. As I reached an intersection a hedge sprang up obscuring my vision and I did not see the other car.'*

☞ *'Coming home I drove into the wrong house and collided with a tree I don't have.'*

☞ *'I thought my window was down, but I found it was up when I put my head through it.'*

☞ *'To avoid hitting the bumper of the car in front I struck a pedestrian.'*

☞ *'My car was legally parked as it backed into another vehicle.'*

☞ *'The pedestrian had no idea which way to run as I ran over him.'*

☞ 'The indirect cause of the accident was a little guy in a small car with a big mouth.'

☞ 'I had been learning to drive with power steering. I turned the wheel to what I thought was enough and found myself in a different direction going the opposite way.'

☞ 'When I saw I could not avoid a collision I stepped on the gas and crashed into the other car.'

☞ 'The accident happened when the right front door of a car came round the corner without giving a signal.'

☞ 'The accident occurred when I was attempting to bring my car out of a skid by steering it into the other vehicle.'

☞ 'I bumped into a lamp-post which was obscured by human beings.'

☞ 'The accident was caused by me waving to the man I hit last week.'

☞ *'The accident was due to the other man narrowly missing me.'*

☞ *'The accident was due to the road bending.'*

☞ *'As I was driving around a bend, one of the doors opened and a frozen kebab flew out, hitting and damaging a passing car.'*

☞ *'The other man altered his mind and I had to run over him.'*

☞ *'If the other driver had stopped a few yards behind himself, it would not have happened.'*

Quotation

'If you don't want to do something, one excuse is as good as another.'
Proverb

☞ *'She suddenly saw me, lost her head and we collided.'*

☞ *'I blew my horn but it would not work as it was stolen.'*

☞ *'I thought the garage had only four posts, but my car bumped into a fifth.'*

☞ 'I left my car unattended for a minute and, whether by accident or design, it ran away.'

And then there are the cows ...

☞ Damage to a car's paintwork was caused, claimed the owner, by a herd of cows licking the car.

☞ When a woman's car ended up in the sea her excuse was that it had been hit by a submarine. The car was parked at the end of the slipway where a submarine was due to berth. Unfortunately the sub collided with the end of the slipway, broke a section off and the car fell into the water. The woman's claim for compensation was paid by the British Navy.

Quotation

'Difficulty is the excuse history never accepts.'
Edward R Murrow

☞ 'A house hit my car' is another strange but true insurance claim excuse. The prefabricated house was being moved by a lorry when it fell off and crushed the car.

☞ A man had an accident on his motorbike and was on his way to hospital. Even though he was hurt, his first thought was to explain to his wife why he'd been in the area where he'd had the accident. He phoned his insurance company and asked them to phone his wife, telling her that he had been kidnapped with his motorbike then dumped on the side of the road. The insurance company told him they didn't dish out excuses for errant husbands, and the man had to come up with his own excuse for his whereabouts.

☞ One driver's excuse for hitting the car in front was that he was unable to brake because a potato had become lodged behind the brake pedal.

☞ Police suspected a black bear of stealing a car in New Jersey, USA. The window and door of the car were damaged, the handbrake had been released and the car ended up 15 metres or so from the owner's house. The damage and, most tellingly, bear fur inside the car pointed to the chief suspect.

Top Ten Motor Accident Excuses

All of these are quotes from insurance claims

1 *'As I approached an intersection a sign suddenly appeared in a place where no stop sign had ever appeared before.'*

2 *'A lamp-post bumped into my car, damaging it in two places.'*

3 *'The telephone pole was approaching. I was attempting to swerve out of the way when I struck the front end.'*

4 *'Three women were talking to each other, and when one stepped back and one stepped forward, I had to have an accident.'*

5 *'A cow wandered into my car. I was afterwards informed that the cow was half witted.'*

6 *'I knocked over a man; he admitted it was his fault for he had been knocked down before.'*

7 *'No one was to blame for the accident but it would never have happened if the other driver had been alert.'*

8 *'In an attempt to kill a fly I drove into a telephone pole.'*

9 *'I consider neither vehicle to blame, but if either was to blame it was the other one.'*

10 *'An invisible car came out of nowhere, struck my car and vanished.'*

Other accident excuses

As with car accidents, no type of accident is ever your fault. There's always someone or something else to blame ...

☞ A man tried to sue the local authority when he soiled his trousers. His claim explained that the authority had closed the bus station toilets, and was therefore responsible for his accident. He demanded the price of a new pair of trousers but was unsuccessful.

Quotation

'Excuses are the nails used to build a house of failure.'
Don Wilder

☞ A bin man asked for compensation from his local authority because he'd suffered shock when a dead badger fell out of a dustbin.

☞ A shoplifter fell down some steps while she was running from the scene of a crime. She tried to sue the shop she'd just stolen from for her accident.

☞ Missing and broken mobile phones account for thousands of insurance claims every year, none of them the fault of the phone's owner. One phone owner was rammed by a sheep in a field, which crushed the phone, another phone was stolen by a magpie (the owner could hear it ringing in a tree), one phone was put into a potty and peed on, and another was eaten by a rabbit.

☞ A driver made a claim for a new windscreen because a frozen squirrel had fallen out of a tree and smashed it.

☞ A homeowner made a claim to recarpet and redecorate his living room: he explained that his pet Labrador had dipped its tail in some white paint, then wagged all over the room while its owners were out.

☞ One man claimed compensation when he sprained his wrist 'while putting sugar on the strawberries'.

Chapter 8

The Balls Were Too Bouncy: Sporting Excuses

Sportsmen and women are competitive people. So when they don't do very well, or things go wrong, someone or something else is usually at fault ...

☞ Formula One driver Nigel Mansell was well in the lead on the final lap of the Canadian Grand Prix, when he unexpectedly slowed to a halt. He had been so confident of winning that he was waving to the crowd and hit the engine's cut-off switch by mistake. He blamed the car, claiming it was too small.

☞ In 1992 Zambian tennis player Lighton Ndefwayl lost a tournament to Musumba Bwayla. He wasn't a very good loser.

Afterwards he outlined the reasons for having lost the match: 'Bwayla is a stupid man and a hopeless player. He has a huge nose and is cross-eyed. Girls hate him. He beat me because my jockstrap was too tight and because when he serves he farts, and that made me lose my concentration, for which I am famous throughout Zambia.'

Quotation

'He who excuses himself accuses himself.'
Gabriel Meurier

☞ Top baseball player Jose Cardenal became famous for his excuses. Before the first game of a new season he said he couldn't play because he had 'slept funny and couldn't blink'. Another time he said the crickets outside his hotel room had kept him awake all night.

☞ US President George W Bush fell off his mountain bike after cycling into a policeman outside the venue for the G8 conference in 2005. His excuse was: 'When you ride a mountain bike, sometimes you fall, otherwise you are not riding hard. The pavement was slick and the bike came off underneath me.' The president crashed his bike at his ranch the year before, in 2003 he fell off a scooter at his house in Maine, and in 2002 he toppled off his sofa in the White House when he choked on a pretzel and fainted.

☞ Snooker player Ronnie O'Sullivan was winning by 8 frames to 3 against Steve Davis in a 1997 final, when play was interrupted by a naked woman, who streaked around the arena before she was captured, covered up and removed. O'Sullivan then lost every one of the next seven frames, and the final – his excuse was that the streaker had broken his concentration. In a different game, O'Sullivan said when he missed an easy shot that he had been distracted by someone in the crowd dressed as a Teletubby.

☞ Hilbert van der Duim fell over during a 10,000-metre speed skating race at the

European Championships and missed out on an expected gold medal. He blamed bird droppings.

☞ Mervyn King, a darts player, lost the world darts championship semi-final in 2003 to Raymond Barneveld and blamed the air conditioning, which he claimed had blown his darts off course. He said, 'I asked for it to be turned off before I went up there and it wasn't. I asked for it to be turned off at the break – it wasn't. The air conditioning doesn't affect Raymond because he throws a heavier dart and a very flat dart.' The organisers of the match said that the air conditioning hadn't been on.

☞ Making excuses for casualties in his sport, boxer Alan Minter said, 'Sure there have been injuries and deaths in boxing, but none of them serious.'

☞ When the Sri Lankan cricket team lost to Pakistan in 2001, their excuse was that their clothes were too tight. Team captain Sanath

Jayasuriya said, 'We had to add extensions to the trousers and the shirts looked more like tight-fitting women's blouses.' He claimed the tight clothing had restricted the players' movement.

☞ The coach of the New Zealand rugby team, Laurie Mains, provided New Zealand's excuse for losing the 1995 World Cup against South Africa: he said many of the players had had food poisoning 48 hours before the match. He even went so far as to blame a waitress for deliberately poisoning the team's water.

☞ Tennis star Venus Williams also used food poisoning as an excuse when she was beaten in the Australian Open by Martina Hingis.

Football

☞ Rotherham goalkeeper Chris Mooney let a goal slip between his legs. His excuse was the glare caused by the centre-half's bald head.

☞ Uruguay beat Scotland 7-0 in the 1954 World Cup. Scottish player Tommy Docherty blamed the length of the Uruguayan national anthem, which he said kept the Scotland players standing still for too long before the start of the game.

☞ In the opening matches of the Euro 2000 football tournament, Holland manager Frank Rijkaard blamed his team's poor performance on too many card games.

☞ In the Euro 2004 football tournament, David Beckham blamed his poor performance on the fitness programme at his club, the hot weather and, when he missed a penalty in the quarter final against Portugal, the condition of the pitch.

☞ Lee Chapman, a Leeds United striker, also blamed the condition of the pitch for missing an easy goal. He said that Hunslet

Quotation

'Bad men excuse their faults; good men abandon them.'

Anonymous

rugby club had churned up the pitch at the Leeds ground, not realising that Hunslet hadn't yet started playing there.

☞ Newcastle United was expected to beat underdog Stevenage in an FA Cup match. Instead they drew. Newcastle's manager, Kenny Dalglish said his team's poor performance was because 'the balls were too bouncy'!

☞ Arsenal beat Liverpool and won the league in 1989, despite needing to win by two clear goals. Liverpool's manager said that the only reason Arsenal had 'achieved the impossible' was because the game had been played on a Friday night. If the teams had played on a Saturday, Liverpool would have won.

Quotation

'A real failure does not need an excuse. It is an end in itself.'
Gertrude Stein

☞ Football manager Alex Ferguson also blamed clothing for his team's defeat. Manchester United was losing 3-0 at half-time against Southampton and Ferguson's excuse was that the players were finding it hard to see one another because they were wearing a grey away kit. During the break the team changed into white shirts but still lost 3-1.

☞ After the Manchester United goalkeeper made a mistake that cost his team a place in the FA Cup, Ferguson blamed the Old Trafford ground: he claimed rugby games played there had spoiled the pitch. Other excuses from Alex Ferguson about Manchester United include too many international fixtures, not enough injury time, biased referees and too many matches.

TOP 20 Top Twenty Football Excuses

1 'An inch or two either side of the post and that would have been a goal.'

Dave Bassett, manager

2 'The shot from Laws was precise but wide.'

Alan Parry, commentator

3 'I would also think that the action replay showed it to be worse than it actually was.'

Ron Atkinson, pundit

4 'This is the fifth refereeing error against us in four games and it's clear now that it's a political issue. Last season there were four left-wing fan groups, Modena, Perugia, Ancona and Empoli, and all four clubs were relegated. They can bring in international referees for our games, but we'd always be penalised because we're left-wing.'

Cristiano Lucarelli, manager

5 'The crowd think that Todd handled the ball ... they must have seen something that nobody else did.'

Barry Davies, commentator

6 'I never comment on referees and I'm not going to break the habit of a lifetime for that prat.'

Ron Atkinson

1 'You can't say my team aren't winners. They've proved that by finishing fourth, third and second in the past three seasons.'

Gerard Houllier, manager

8 'There was nothing wrong with the performance, apart from throwing away the game.'

Glenn Hoddle, manager

9 'We actually got the winner three minutes from the end but then they equalised.'

Ian McNail, manager

10 'If that had gone in, it would have been a goal.'

David Coleman, commentator

11 'Woodcock would have scored but his shot was too perfect.'

Ron Atkinson

12 'I'd been ill and hadn't trained for a week and I'd been out of the team for three weeks before that, so I wasn't sharp. I got cramp before half-time as well. But I'm not one to make excuses.'

Clinton Morrison, player

13 'That was the perfect penalty, apart from he missed it.'

Rob McCaffrey, presenter

14 'I'm not trying to make excuses for David Seaman but I think the lights may have been a problem.'

Kevin Keegan, manager

15 'Without being too harsh on David, he cost us the match.'

Ian Wright, player

16 'We haven't been scoring goals, but football's not just about scoring goals. It's about winning.'

Alan Shearer, player

17 'We lost the FA Cup because our kits were too heavy for such a hot day.'

Emlyn Hughes, player

'We conceded a goal which was clearly offside and then one from a clear foul on our goalkeeper.'

Dror Kashtan, manager

 'The weather was too hot and my team are not used to this hot weather.'

Gianluca Vialli, manager

 'Of the ten sendings-off, nine have been different players, so it proves we're unlucky.'

Keith Stevens, manager

Quotation

'Don't do what you'll have to find an excuse for.'

Proverb

Drugs tests

☞ American cyclist Floyd Landis won the 2006 Tour de France but was found guilty of cheating and disqualified when he failed a drugs test afterwards, which showed high levels of the male hormone testosterone. He insisted that he was innocent and said he must have naturally high testosterone levels –

but no one, no matter how manly, has levels as high as *that.* The other excuses he made included an injection for a bad hip, a beer and a whisky the night before, thyroid medication, and taking an unknown substance without realising that it affected the result of the test. Despite all the excuses, the drug test result wasn't overturned.

☞ An Australian netball player, Carol Gaudie, also failed a drugs test for testosterone. Her excuse was that her drink must have been spiked while she was at a nightclub the night before. She didn't come up with a reason why anyone would *want* to spike a drink with an artificial male hormone, though.

☞ When sprinter Justin Gatlin tested positive for testosterone, his coach explained that Gatlin had been set up: his masseuse had rubbed testosterone cream into the runner's legs without him knowing about it.

☞ Shane Warne, the Australian cricketer, failed a drugs test for a different banned substance.

His excuse was that his mum had given him a diet tablet that contained the drug because he wanted to look thinner on the telly.

☞ In the 1988 Olympics, sprinter Ben Johnson tested positive for steroids. He denied taking them and insisted that his energy drink had been spiked.

☞ Snowboarder Ross Rebagliati had his Olympic gold taken away after testing positive for another banned drug. His excuse was passive smoking at a friend's party. Eventually, Rebagliati did get his medal back and promised to wear a gas mask to parties in future.

☞ Baseball player Rafael Palmeiro implied that a drug was present in his body by mysterious means: 'I am sure you will ask how I tested positively for a banned substance. As I look back, I don't have a specific answer to give. I wasn't able to explain how the banned substance entered my body.'

☞ Tennis player Petr Korda tested positive for a steroid which is also used to fatten animals. Korda's excuse was that he had eaten a lot of veal recently. Tennis officials estimated that Korda would have needed to eat 40 calves a day for 20 years for there to be such high levels of the drug in his body.

☞ Long-distance runner Dieter Baumann tested positive for the same steroid and blamed his toothpaste, which he claimed had been spiked by a rival.

☞ Football player Rio Ferdinand didn't turn up for a routine drugs test and was fined and banned from playing for eight months. His excuse was that he forgot – he was preoccupied with buying bed linen.

Team Efforts

☞ The Ukrainian football team lost to Spain 4-0 at the 2006 World Cup and came up with an unusual excuse: noisy frogs outside the team's hotel room. 'Because of the frogs' croaking we hardly got a wink of sleep,' one player explained.

☞ Most of the Kent cricket team were hours late for a match at the Oval against Surrey because of a burst water main five miles away. The car journey from their hotel to the Oval should have taken 15 minutes but ended up taking two hours. The captain arrived on time because he lived in London and travelled by public transport from a different direction. Another player made it after getting out of his team mate's car and taking the tube. At least they all had the same excuse.

☞ The England cricket team made their lowest ever Test score in South Africa in 1999. They blamed low cloud.

☞ During the 2004 Athens Olympics, the team from Finland didn't win many medals. Excuses from Finnish athletes included being surprised by the size of the stadium (from javelin thrower Paula Huhtaniemi), a different masseuse (from runner Kirsi Valsti) and, from sailor Sari Multala, a bag caught in the back of the boat.

☞ During the same Olympic Games, Indian athletes were full of excuses too. The hockey team blamed the umpire, Anju Bobby George blamed her poor performance in the long jump on high levels of pollution in Athens, weight-lifter Karnam Malleswari had a bad back, markswoman Anjali Bhagwat had aching muscles, runner KM Binu put the wrong shoes on, and markswoman Suma Shirur went to pieces because she was stunned by the size of the Olympic Games event.

Chapter 9

It Wasn't My Fault: Excuses for Behaving Badly

Everyone behaves badly from time to time. Some people do the decent thing: they hang their heads in shame and apologise. Others try to weasel their way out of it with excuses.

Crimes and Misdemeanours

☞ An eight-year-old boy arrived home from school driving his teacher's car because, he said, he hadn't felt like walking home. The boy, from Hungary, wasn't charged with theft but he was expelled from school.

☞ A man began throwing objects and finally clothes out of his moving truck, before stopping the truck and running naked along the road past a police station. He was captured and arrested. His excuse was that he'd just been to the dentist and had taken too many painkillers.

☞ You'd think there would be no excuse for driving a car while drunk, but a Canadian driver who was stopped by police told them he was speeding and drunk because he believed the singer Shania Twain was helping him drive. In court, a judge ruled that the man wasn't responsible because he suffered from delusions about telepathic communication from female celebrities.

☞ With some people it's *any* excuse, and with one Florida man it was chilli sauce. The man wanted 10 sachets of chilli sauce with his order in a fast-food restaurant but the cashier told him she could only hand out three. When the manager appeared, the customer shot him several times, and he was lucky to recover later on in hospital. Ironically, the manager had already put 11 packets of chilli sauce in the customer's bag.

☞ When the actress Winona Ryder was caught shoplifting, she claimed it was all part of research for her role. She said, 'I was told that I should shoplift. The director said I should try it out,' according to a security guard at Saks in New York.

☞ An art college student was always breaking classroom rules. When her teacher pointed out that there was a sign with the rules on it on the wall of the classroom, she replied, 'I don't take any notice of that sign – it's a yucky green colour.'

☞ A woman from Iowa, USA, pretended to be dead so that she didn't have to pay a parking fine. She forged various documents and a letter to a judge that said she had died in a car crash. The woman was found out when she was stopped for another traffic offence a month after her 'death'.

☞ When you're caught red-handed there's no excuse. A Russian man offered a police officer £1,200 to drop the case against him. When the policeman refused, the man began eating the money in a desperate attempt to destroy the evidence that he was guilty of bribery as well.

☞ At the Live 8 concert in 2005 the audience booed Pete Doherty's performance: he stumbled about the stage and forgot the words to a song. His excuse was that Peaches Geldof had pinched his bum just before he walked on stage, which 'did my head in'.

> **Quotation**
>
> 'We excuse our sloth under the pretext of difficulty.'
>
> Marcus Fabius Quintilian

☞ An Austrian student began throwing furniture out of a third-floor window on a hot summer's day. The whole street had to be cordoned off as chairs, tables and even a bed were thrown on to the pavement, until the

21-year-old man was finally restrained. His excuse was heatstroke – apparently this had 'affected his emotional state'.

☞ There is never a satisfactory excuse for double-parking: funeral cars were fined in East London even though they had a perfectly good one – that their drivers were too busy carrying the coffin to the hearse to move their cars.

☞ A student didn't have a lot of necessary art materials. His excuse to his teacher was that he couldn't buy any because his parents wouldn't give him the money – they thought he'd spend it on cigarettes. His teacher helpfully suggested that he could show his parents the art materials to prove how he'd spent the money. 'Nah,' the student replied, 'it's too tempting to spend it on ciggies.'

☞ A woman explained to an inspector that she didn't have a TV licence because she didn't have a TV, though the inspector could see one behind her. He asked her about it and she told him it was broken. But the inspector had noticed a red light on the TV's control panel. The woman explained: 'Oh, that wee red light. I just keep that on as it keeps the damp from getting into it.'

☞ One woman had no excuse: an inspector visited a house that didn't have a TV licence but got no reply. He called back later on and found someone else already at the door. When no one answered the doorbell, the visitor shouted through the letter box, 'It's OK, it's not the TV licensing man,' and the door was opened. The woman who opened the door then asked who the inspector was, and was told, 'I'm the TV licensing man.'

☞ An American pilot flying in Soviet air space was captured and charged with spying. When he was returned to the US, he explained: 'I was a pilot flying an airplane and it just so happened that where I was flying made what I was doing spying.'

You see? It could happen to anyone.

☞ A trouserless policeman had an odd but absolutely true excuse for his appearance: his trousers had been ripped off by an emu. The policeman had been trying to catch the bird, which had been alarming people in a park in Germany.

☞ A mother in Croatia made excuses for her ten-year-old son's bad marks at school by saying that the headmaster and his wife had a personal vendetta against her son and had told the other teachers to give him bad marks. She even took the teachers to court in order to try and prove it. Teachers at the school said that the child had been given bad marks because he had done badly at his subjects.

☞ There's no excuse for forgetting your children's birthdays but one Welsh mum kept forgetting her five kids' special days. To make sure she remembered she had their initials and dates of birth tattooed on her arms.

Emergency!

Ever since the emergency number 999 was started in the UK in 1937 there have been time-wasting calls from hoaxers and idiots. In fact as much as 40% of calls to the emergency services are not real emergencies. Here are some of the most stupid and strange excuses for making 999 calls that have been recorded over the years:

☞ A woman phoned because she had shampoo in her eyes.

☞ A man asked for help with the crossword.

☞ Several calls ordered takeaway food or asked for delivery of takeaways.

☞ Someone else had a broken fingernail.

☞ Several calls demanded help changing the TV channel.

☞ A man called because he had had a *dream* that

he had collapsed and was lying unconscious.

☞ Someone reported 'a large owl sitting on a telegraph pole'.

☞ A man wanted help getting a drink from the fridge.

☞ The North East Ambulance Service has reported several incidents of people phoning for an ambulance and faking injuries when they were having trouble finding a taxi, assuming (wrongly) that the ambulance would then take them home.

☞ A woman asked for help getting her drunk boyfriend upstairs to bed.

☞ An angry neighbour reported a baby crying.

☞ Another angry neighbour reported builders making too much noise.

☞ A woman phoned because her trousers didn't fit.

☞ A man reported a pigeon in his back garden.

From around the world...

Emergency!

☞ A woman called 911 from a US restaurant because her onion rings were cold and the waiter refused to replace them.

☞ The German emergency service line was plagued by calls from a man who said he had fallen in love with the operator's voice.

☞ An elderly lady in Italy called out police on an 'emergency' but they arrived to discover that her TV set had broken down during an episode of her favourite soap.

☞ An eldery lady called the police in North Carolina because a local takeaway wouldn't deliver pizza to her house and she wanted them arrested.

☞ Three police cars turned up in New Jersey after tracing a series of late-night 911 calls. A woman said that she'd been teaching her dog to dial 911 by knocking the receiver off the hook then pressing the numbers with his paw.

People who should know better

☞ David Dinkins, mayor of New York City, had failed to pay his income tax for five years. He explained, 'I haven't committed a crime. What I did was fail to comply with the law.'

☞ At the 60th anniversary meeting of the United Nations, the biggest ever gathering of national leaders, President George W Bush excused himself to go to the toilet.

☞ Politicians have been known to make excuses for not doing more to reduce pollution. US President Ronald Reagan said: 'I have flown twice over Mount St Helens [a volcano] out on our west coast. I'm not a scientist and I don't know the figures, but I have a suspicion that that one little mountain has probably released more sulphur dioxide into the atmosphere of the world than has been released in the last ten years of automobile driving or things of that kind that people are so concerned about.' He made even less sense when he said, 'Trees cause more pollution than automobiles do.' And Dan Quayle pointed out that, 'It isn't pollution that's harming the environment. It's impurities in our air and water that are doing it.'

☞ Mexican politician Roberto Madrazo had

suffered defeat in the country's general election. Soon afterwards he clocked an amazing time in the Berlin Marathon and came top of his age group. But questions were raised and Madrazo was found to have taken a shortcut. His excuse was that he'd been injured and headed straight to the finish line to pick up his clothes and participatory medal. Not many people believed him, since he'd run across the finish line waving his arms in the air.

☞ 'It depends on your definition of asleep. They were not stretched out. They had their eyes closed. They were seated at their desks with their heads in a nodding position.'

Quotation
'Every vice has its excuse ready.'
Publius Syrus

John Hogan, Supervisor of News Information, responding to a charge that two nuclear plant workers were asleep at work.

☞ 'He didn't say that. He was reading what was given to him in a speech.'

Company director Richard Darman, making excuses for President George W Bush when it became clear the president wasn't fulfilling a pledge to save wetlands.

☞ 'I didn't accept it. I received it.'

Richard Allen, National Security Advisor to President Reagan, explaining the money and gifts he'd been given by Japanese journalists after he arranged a private interview for them with First Lady Nancy Reagan.

☞ 'Outside of the killings, Washington has one of the lowest crime rates in the country.'

Mayor Marion Barry, Washington, DC

☞ 'Sure, it's going to kill a lot of people, but they may be dying of something else anyway.'

Othal Brand, member of a Texas review board, on a chemical used in pesticides.

☞ 'Reports that say that something hasn't

happened are always interesting to me, because as we know, there are "known knowns"; there are things we know we know. We also know there are "known unknowns"; that is to say we know there are some things we do not know. But there are also "unknown unknowns" – the ones we don't know we don't know.'

Donald Rumsfeld, US Defence Secretary

☞ 'The streets are safe in Philadelphia. It's only the people who make them unsafe.'

Frank Rizzo, Mayor of Philadelphia

Speeding

☞ The football manager Alex Ferguson has made lots of excuses for his team, but he also managed to come up with an excuse for speeding that was

Quotation
'Several excuses are always less convincing than one.'
Aldous Huxley

good enough to get him cleared of the offence in 1999: diarrhoea. He said, 'I had to go somewhere quickly.'

☞ Police reported that several different van drivers in Cambridge all gave the excuse that their vans had to go over the speed limit when travelling uphill. The excuse didn't get them off and they were still fined.

☞ Another motorist claimed that he was rushing some severed fingers to hospital: his friend had just accidentally chopped them off.

☞ Speed cameras allow speeding drivers to concoct excuses without having to reveal any evidence, as the drivers would if they'd been pulled over for speeding by a policeman.

Excuses given include various ailing pets that need to be rushed to the vet's: dogs, cats, hamsters, guinea pigs, budgies, a parrot and an iguana have been named – and no doubt countless others.

☞ A car driver stopped for speeding in South Wales made the excuse that he was driving an unfamiliar car and the speedometer was in a different position from the one he was used to, so he was looking at the rev counter by mistake. He was still fined.

☞ Although it seems unlikely that anyone could really be this stupid, a policeman in Michigan claimed that he stopped a car that was more than 25 mph over the speed limit. The driver explained that there had been a bee buzzing around his head, so he sped up hoping that the bee couldn't fly that fast and would be stuck in the back seat.

☞ Another really stupid excuse: 'I didn't think the speed limit applied after midnight.'

☞ And yet another one: a traffic officer in Florida pulled over a driver who was speeding along at 95 mph. The driver's excuse was that he'd seen a sign with the speed limit on it – 95. He was talking about the name of the road, the I (interstate) 95.

☞ A driver in Northumbria came up with another original excuse when he was caught on a speed camera: 'I had passed out after seeing flashing lights, which I believed to be UFOs in the distance. The flash of the camera brought me round from my trance.'

☞ A Swiss man blamed the lack of goats on the road when he was caught speeding on a Canadian road. He said he was 35 mph over the speed limit because 'of the ability to go faster without risking hitting a goat', apparently a common problem on roads in Switzerland. The policeman who stopped him was impressed by the originality of the excuse but the man was still ordered to pay a fine.

Other speed camera excuses include:

☞ *'I was under the airport's flight path and I believe the camera was triggered by a jet overhead, not my car.'*

☞ *'There was a strong wind behind my car which pushed me over the limit.'*

☞ *'The vibrations from the surfboard I had on the roof rack set off the camera.'*

☞ *'A violent sneeze caused a chain reaction where my foot pushed down harder on the accelerator.'*

☞ *'The only way I could demonstrate my faulty clutch was to accelerate madly.'*

☞ *'My ex-girlfriend still has keys to my car and keeps taking it without asking. I didn't report this to the police.'*

☞ *'I was trying to sell my car and the person who was clocked by a speed camera was test driving the vehicle.'*

☞ *'I picked up a hitchhiker who commented that*

they liked my car so I let this person drive the vehicle. I don't have their name or address.'

☞ *'My car was stolen overnight and returned to the same point. I didn't report this to the police, as the first thing I knew of the matter was when a notice of intended prosecution for speeding came through my door.'*

☞ *'As I entered on to the motorway, my car was dragged along in the slip stream of a truck. My brakes aren't very good, so I had to keep pace with it.'*

☞ An Illinois policeman pulled over a driver who had run a red light even though there had been plenty of time to stop. The driver's excuse was that she had just had her brakes repaired and didn't want to wear them down.

☞ A Finnish traffic officer gave a driver a parking ticket. He was surprised to hear the driver's excuse: that he had been hypnotised into parking illegally.

Behaving Badly at Work

☞ When all the pipes froze at a small company in California, the boss refused to hire an emergency portable toilet. He explained that he couldn't afford it because he and his wife were spending a lot of money on buying a new house – just one chandelier cost $20,000.

☞ A teacher at a primary school in Austria gave homework on swear words to a class of nine-year-olds. He was sacked despite his excuse that he was trying to show children which words should not be used.

☞ If you have to make excuses on your CV, you know you're in trouble. One CV read, 'The company made me a scapegoat – just like my three previous employers.' And another, 'Please don't misconstrue my 14 jobs as "job-hopping". I have never quit a job.'

☞ A man stole £5 million from the security company he worked for in Germany. When he was caught with the money stuffed into the boot of his car, he said he'd stolen it because he'd worked hard for the company but had never been given a pay rise. The excuse didn't do him much good: he ended up in prison for four years.

☞ A man shamelessly used his own mother's death as an excuse to borrow money from his boss, saying he needed the money to pay for her funeral. In fact his mother was alive and well, as his boss found out almost immediately when the man's mother visited him at work just a few moments after he'd told his boss she was dead. The man was promptly given the sack. You would think there wouldn't be any excuse in those circumstances, but the sacked man came up with one: he said that someone had phoned him and told him his mother had died – though he couldn't say who the person was. No one believed his story.

Quotation

'Any excuse will serve a tyrant.'

Aesop

☞ One man went back to work after a holiday to discover he'd lost his job because he'd been declared dead. When the man assured his boss he was in perfect health he was given an apology and the excuse of 'a computer error'. But he was told he couldn't have his job back because someone else had already been employed to replace him.

Could the whole explanation have been an elaborate excuse to get rid of him?

☞ An office manager embezzled $3.7 million from the company she worked for in Seattle,

USA. She spent the money on 32 cars, more than 600 Barbie dolls, and 192 pieces of jewellery, among other things. Her excuse: compulsive shopping.

☞ A man in Moldova claimed his wife had died in a car accident in order to borrow money from his workmates, telling them he needed the cash for the funeral. His helpful friends raised about £3,000, then called at his house to see if there was anything else they could do ... and the 'dead' woman opened the door. The man was arrested when his shameless excuse was exposed.

☞ A teacher from Illinois, USA, falsely claimed to be seriously ill and defrauded her colleagues of $37,000. Her defence lawyer's excuse was, 'This was a situation where she couldn't stand the pressure of opportunity.'

☞ Admiral H G Rickover of the US Navy had a notice pinned to his office door that dissuaded people from giving excuses. It read:

To save time for me and yourself, give your excuse by numbers:

1 I thought I told you.

2 That's the way we've always done it.

3 No one told me to go ahead.

4 I didn't think it was that important.

5 I'm so busy I just couldn't get around to it.

6 Why bother? The Admiral won't buy it.

7 I didn't know you were in a hurry for it.

8 That's his job, not mine.

9   I forgot.

10   I'm waiting for the OK.

11   That's not my department.

12   How did I know this was different?

13   Wait until the boss comes back and ask him.